THIRSTY **HEART**

NOURISHMENT FOR A DEHYDRATED SOUL

STUDY GUIDE

REGINA FOREST

Publisher: Planted Press
ISBN-13: 978-0997949810 (Planted Press)
ISBN-10: 0997949813

Cover Design: Trent Meistrell and Jason Darrah
Interior design and layout: Fusion Creative Works, www.fusioncw.com

Follow at:
Thirstyheartbook.com
Facebook: Thirsty Heart, Regina Forest
Instagram: @thirstyheartbook, @reg4est
Twitter: @ReginaForest
Blog: reg4est.wordpress.com
Bridgerelationships.com

Oftentimes heart dehydration can sneak up on you. Sometimes you can be walking down life's road unaware of your heart's thirst. Other times, you may have an understanding that something is just not right but might not be able to pinpoint the issue. Please be encouraged to drink deeper of heart hydration by using this study guide in conjunction with the book *Thirsty Heart*.

You can find the answers to most questions in the book, corresponding with sections in each chapter. Some of the answers will require a time of reflection because they will be specific to your journey. Feel free to use this for personal study or in a group setting.

Enjoy!

CONTENTS

For I will pour water on him who is thirsty,
And floods on the dry ground.

—Isaiah 44:3a

1
HEART HYDRATION

If there is lack or dehydration in your heart, soul or life, then one or more of the issues listed below may be the cause. Recognition of your issue is the first step to heart hydration. Underline the ones that apply to you.

- lack an intimate relationship with Jesus
- struggle with your identity in Christ
- never feel good enough for God
- struggle to understand God's grace
- hold a grudge against God
- live outside the provision of the cross
- struggle with selfishness
- have trouble with submission
- struggle to make Jesus enough
- have weak faith, trust, or belief
- struggle to be thankful
- struggle with love and obedience
- are brokenhearted
- struggle with forgiveness
- suffer from sexual brokenness
- feel damaged from the messiness of life

1. What is the cure for heart dehydration?

_____

_____

_____

_____

2. Why is going to church or doing "Christian stuff" not the answer to heart hydration?

_____

_____

_____

_____

_____

THE BOTTOM LINE

3. What is the bottom line of heart hydration? Why?

_____

_____

_____

_____

_____

PERFECT LOVE

4. What does it mean for you personally to be loved unconditionally by Jesus?

_____

_____

_____

_____

_____

5. Read 1 John 4:8 and 1 Corinthians 13:4-7 in different translations. What do these verses tell you about God?

_____

_____

_____

_____

_____

6. Read Ephesians 3:14–19. What is Paul praying for believers? If you struggle with stepping into and receiving God's love, make these Scriptures your prayer.

_____

_____

_____

_____

_____

7. What does compartmentalizing Jesus mean? Can you identify any areas in your life where you compartmentalize Him?

_____

_____

_____

_____

_____

8. Is Jesus just an addition to your life, or is He your very life?

_____

_____

_____

_____

_____

9.   How will falling in love with Jesus make heart hydration easier?

_____

_____

_____

_____

_____

_____

RELATIONSHIP—RELIGION—RULES

10.   Are you uncomfortable with the idea of having an intimate personal relationship with Jesus? Why or why not? List the three ways mentioned on how to have a real, personal, intimate relationship with Jesus.

_____

_____

_____

_____

_____

_____

11.   If you spent the same amount of time with the person you love as you do with Jesus, would that relationship be very healthy?

_____

_____

_____

_____

_____

_____

12. How will you train yourself to know that Jesus is always with you? How can you be intentional not to ignore Him?

_____

_____

_____

_____

_____

_____

_____

13. Why is it important to read the Bible daily? Do you have a designated time every day when you read the Bible? If not, when will you start?

_____

_____

_____

_____

_____

_____

_____

14. Read 1 Thessalonians 5:17. What does it mean to pray without ceasing? Are your prayers a dialogue or monologue? If a monologue, what will you do to change this?

_____

_____

_____

_____

_____

_____

_____

15. What is the difference between living in a relationship with Jesus versus living by a set of rules? In what ways do religion and rules cause heart dehydration?

_____

_____

_____

_____

16. Read Galatians 5:1–4 and Galatians 2:21. What do these Scriptures tell you about living by the rules? What truth do they tell you about living free?

_____

_____

_____

_____

17. What is the difference between an obedience-based relationship and a performance-based one? Which one applies more to you?

_____

_____

_____

_____

18. Pray and ask Jesus to help you fall in love with Him. Invite Him into your heart and ask Him to help you know Him intimately. Write out your prayer.

_____

_____

_____

_____

_____

2

KNOW WHO YOU ARE

THE SIMPLE TRUTH ABOUT LIES

1. What is one of the main ways the enemy of your soul tries to influence your life? Who does he lie to you about?

    _____

    _____

    _____

    _____

2. What are three of the ways lies can present themselves to you? What is the best way to fight and avoid lies?

    _____

    _____

    _____

    _____

3. Why is it important to ask Jesus to give you discernment?

    _____

    _____

    _____

    _____

4.   Write down the quick and simple formula for addressing lies.

_____

_____

_____

_____

_____

5.   How does this formula work?

_____

_____

_____

_____

_____

THE EXCHANGE

6.   What does 2 Corinthians 5:21 tell you about who God is and what He has done?

_____

_____

_____

_____

_____

7.   Explain the Great Exchange.

_____

_____

_____

_____

_____

8.   How do you implement the concept of exchange into your
     life daily?

_____

_____

_____

_____

DEAD TO SIN

9.   Read Romans 6:4–11. List at least ten points from this
     Scripture that tell you about who you are in Christ.

_____

_____

_____

_____

_____

_____

10. Read Romans 6:12–14, Galatians 5:17, and Romans 7:14–
     24. What do these three Scriptures tell you about the strug-
     gle of accepting the truth about living a resurrected life?

_____

_____

_____

_____

11. Read Romans 7:24–25 and 8:1–3. What is the answer to
     our dilemma of the human condition?

_____

_____

_____

_____

HIDDEN IN CHRIST

12. Read Colossians 3:1–3. What does it mean to be hidden in Christ?

_____

_____

_____

_____

_____

_____

CREATED FOR A PURPOSE

13. Do you believe you were created for a purpose? Do you believe you have great value and potential? If not, what will you do about it?

_____

_____

_____

_____

_____

_____

14. How does knowing who you are in Christ help you avoid a performance-based life of continually striving?

_____

_____

_____

_____

_____

_____

15. What is oppression? Can you identify any areas in your life where there is oppression? Read Isaiah 54:14. What does it say about oppression? Do you believe this Scripture as your present-day truth?

_____

_____

_____

_____

_____

_____

16. Read Galatians 4:7, 2 Corinthians 5:21, Colossians 2:9–10, and Ephesians 2:6. What do these Scriptures say about who you are? If you struggle to believe and own these truths, please make these Scriptures your prayer.

_____

_____

_____

_____

_____

_____

17. What is your position as a believer in Christ? As a believer, how much access do you have to the heart of God?

_____

_____

_____

_____

_____

_____

QUALIFIED

18. Can you identify any areas in your life where the enemy tries to disqualify you? Can you see areas where you have disqualified yourself?

_____
_____
_____
_____
_____

19. Why is it important to know who you are in Christ? Please take the time to pray and ask Jesus to help you believe the truth about who He is in you, and who you are in Him. Ask Him to reveal any lies that you have believed about Him and about yourself. List them. As He exposes falsehoods, please follow the quick and simple formula mentioned earlier on how to deal with lies:
    • Recognize
    • Exchange
    • Believe

_____
_____
_____
_____
_____
_____
_____

3
STEP INTO IT

1. Would you say you are living in the fullness of all Christ has provided for you?

    _____

    _____

    _____

    _____

2. Can you relate to the son in this allegory? Why or why not?

    _____

    _____

    _____

    _____

3. In what areas of your life are you "living on the lawn" of Jesus' generous provision for you personally?

    _____

    _____

    _____

    _____

4.   Are you content to just admire God's Word and never live in
     its fullness? Why or why not?

_____

_____

_____

_____

_____

5.   What are the listed provisions of the cross?

_____

_____

_____

_____

_____

6.   This provision is all yours—paid in full. The key is in your
     hand. What are the three things you need to do to take
     possession?

_____

_____

_____

_____

_____

STOP LIVING ON THE LAWN

7.   What two things will keep you in bondage and cause you to
     admire the provision from afar?

_____

_____

_____

_____

8. Why is living on the lawn a symptom of a dehydrated heart?

    _____

    _____

    _____

    _____

    _____

9. Read 1 Corinthians 1:27. How does this Scripture relate to living in the provision of the cross?

    _____

    _____

    _____

    _____

    _____

    _____

10. What will it take for you to get off the lawn of your relationship with Jesus and step into all He has provided for you?

    _____

    _____

    _____

    _____

    _____

11. Pray and ask Jesus to give you the courage to step into the fullness of what He has for you. Write out your prayer.

    _____

    _____

    _____

    _____

    _____

12. Please reread the last four paragraphs of chapter 3. Can you relate to any of the issues listed?

_____

_____

_____

_____

_____

_____

13. If you struggle to understand or receive the gifts of grace and the cross, ask Jesus to renew your mind and change your heart about grace.

_____

_____

_____

_____

_____

_____

4

THE "ME" FACTOR

1. Read Romans 8:7–8. What is the Me factor?

    _____
    _____
    _____
    _____
    _____
    _____
    _____
    _____

2. Read Matthew 6:33. What is the kingdom of God? What does it mean to seek first the kingdom of God?

    _____
    _____
    _____
    _____
    _____
    _____
    _____
    _____

IT'S A HEART ISSUE

3. Seeking a heart change is as easy as turning to Jesus and making an exchange with Him. Read Ezekiel 36:25–27 in *The Message*. What does this Scripture tell you about a heart change?

_____

_____

_____

_____

_____

4. Do you need a change of heart to abandon the Me factor? If so, make the exchange now: give Jesus your resistance in trade for a willingness to let go of self.

_____

_____

_____

_____

_____

CLUTTER

5. Can you identify your heart's clutter? Ask God to reveal the clutter in your life. Make a list of what you need to discard.

_____

_____

_____

_____

THE "S" WORD—SUBMIT

6. What does submission mean? Why is submission beneficial to heart hydration?

_____

_____

_____

_____

_____

_____

7. In what ways does living a submitted lifestyle help you live in grace and freedom?

_____

_____

_____

_____

_____

8. Submission as a lifestyle is rooted in what three concepts?

_____

_____

_____

_____

_____

9. What is the difference between surrender and submission?

_____

_____

_____

_____

SUBMIT AND RESIST

10. Read James 4:6–8 and fill in the blanks. "God resists the
     _____, but _____ _____ to the humble. Therefore
     _____ to God. _____ the devil and ___ _____
     _____ from you. _____ _____ to God and _____ ____
     draw near to you."

11. What is the dynamic of James 4:6–8? How does it work in
     the life of a believer?

     _____

     _____

     _____

     _____

     _____

     _____

12. One of the best ways to start your day is to pray through
     James 4:6–8, submitting your heart and soul to Jesus. Why
     is it a good idea to make this your daily practice?

     _____

     _____

     _____

     _____

     _____

13. Thirty-Day Challenge: For thirty days straight, before you
     even get out of bed, turn James 4:6–8 into your prayer and
     submit your heart, soul, and life to Jesus. Throughout your
     day, remind your heart and soul that you are choosing to live
     under God's mission for your life. At the end of the thirty
     days, take note of how you have changed. If this works for
     you, continue with it as a part of your lifestyle.

THE HEART AND SOUL

14. Read Proverbs 4:23, Jeremiah 17:9, 1 Kings 8:39, and Ephesians 3:17. What do these Scriptures tell you about the heart?

_____

_____

_____

_____

_____

_____

_____

15. Read John 5:30. What does it say Jesus did with His will?

_____

_____

_____

_____

_____

_____

16. Read Ephesians 4:22–23, Romans 12:2, and 2 Corinthians 10:5. According to these Scriptures, what do you need to do with your mind? What is the action of bringing every thought into captivity and renewing and transforming your mind?

_____

_____

_____

_____

_____

_____

17.   Should your emotions control the way you live? Should you be in control of your emotions?

_____

_____

_____

_____

_____

_____

_____

18.   Read Galatians 5:22–23. What are the character traits (fruit) that should guide your life? How can you make these your character traits?

_____

_____

_____

_____

_____

_____

_____

HEARING GOD'S VOICE

19.   What is your greatest opposition to hearing God's voice? Why is it important to hear and know His voice?

_____

_____

_____

_____

_____

20. What does it mean to practice God's presence?

_____
_____
_____
_____
_____
_____

GRAVE CLOTHES

21. What do the grave clothes represent?

_____
_____
_____
_____
_____

22. As a believer, as the Bride of Christ, what attire did the cross purchase for you? What do you need to do to wear this attire?

_____
_____
_____
_____
_____
_____

23. Read Galatians 2:20. How does it relate to the Me factor?

_____
_____
_____
_____

THE GRACE AND RIGHTEOUSNESS FACTOR

24.   What part does the Me factor play in living for God?

_____

_____

_____

_____

_____

25.   What is the unearned divine help God gives believers? Why do you need it?

_____

_____

_____

_____

_____

26.   Reread Matthew 6:33. Why do you think it says to seek righteousness if we are already made righteous by Jesus' work on the cross?

_____

_____

_____

_____

27.   What can help you abandon the Me factor, discard your heart's clutter, and step out of grave clothes? Hint: the answer starts with an "S."

_____

_____

_____

_____

_____

28. Can you identify the Me factor in your life? What is it? Pray and ask Jesus for the grace to abandon the Me factor. Ask Him for a change of heart regarding submission. Write out your prayer.

_____

_____

_____

_____

_____

_____

_____

_____

5
JESUS IS ENOUGH

1. Read John 6:35. What does "Jesus is enough" mean? How does this Scripture sum up the phrase "Jesus is enough"? How does it relate to heart hydration?

    _____

    _____

    _____

    _____

    _____

    _____

HOW JESUS BECAME ENOUGH

2. Can you relate to this statement? "No, Lord, you are not enough. But I want you to be." Do you want Jesus to be enough for you? What will you do to make Him enough?

    _____

    _____

    _____

    _____

    _____

    _____

3. What is the meaning of the term "relinquish"? How does it relate to Jesus being enough?

    _____

    _____

    _____

    _____

    _____

4. Do you struggle with trusting Jesus? In what ways?

    _____

    _____

    _____

    _____

5. Is your heart in agreement with the following statement: "Jesus knows trusting Him and letting Him be in charge is the best scenario for your life"? Why or why not?

    _____

    _____

    _____

    _____

    _____

6. What does it mean for you, personally, to come to the end of yourself?

    _____

    _____

    _____

    _____

WHAT ABOUT "ME"?

7. Read Mark 12:29–31. How does this Scripture relate to Jesus being enough?

    _____

    _____

    _____

    _____

    _____

8. What is the loudest, most demanding question people face when loving others as themselves?

    _____

    _____

    _____

    _____

    _____

9. What is always the answer to the *What about Me?* question?

    _____

    _____

    _____

    _____

ENOUGH IS ENOUGH

10. Read Psalm 23:1. What is needed to make this Scripture work?

    _____

    _____

    _____

    _____

11. How does submission relate to Jesus being enough?

_____

_____

_____

_____

12. Read Psalm 33:22 and Psalm 62:5. How do these Scriptures relate to the truth that Jesus is all you need?

_____

_____

_____

_____

HOW IT WORKS

13. Read 2 Corinthians 12:9. How does this Scripture relate to Jesus being enough?

_____

_____

_____

_____

HOW TO KNOW IF JESUS IS NOT ENOUGH

14. What do you reach for in hard times or when you are having a rough day? How can Jesus be enough for you in those situations?

_____

_____

_____

_____

15.   What are your pursuits? Can you see how pursuits can take the place of God in your life? How? What are you driven by? How does this challenge you?

_____

_____

_____

_____

_____

16.   Can you identify the areas in your life where Jesus is not enough? What are they? Can you stretch beyond what is easy and comfortable and ask Jesus to complete you in these areas?

_____

_____

_____

_____

_____

17.   Pray and tell Jesus the truth about Him being enough for you. If need be, ask for a willing heart to make Him enough. Write out your prayer.

_____

_____

_____

_____

_____

6

FAITH IS ESSENTIAL

1. What is an essential piece to quenching a thirsty heart?

_____

_____

_____

_____

_____

_____

2. Can you identify with self (heart)-protection, where you build walls around your heart to protect yourself from getting hurt? If so, what is your reason for protecting your heart? How has this dehydrated your heart? How does it affect your faith?

_____

_____

_____

_____

_____

_____

3.   What is the basic definition of faith for a follower of Christ? Can you take God's Word at face value? Why or why not?

_____

_____

_____

_____

TRUST

4.   What is the definition of trust? Why is trust an essential element in life? Why is trust vital for a believer?

_____

_____

_____

_____

_____

5.   Is trust a choice? Are you willing to make the choice to fully trust God?

_____

_____

_____

_____

UNBELIEF AND TRUE FAITH IN GOD

6.   What is a deadly cancer to the heart of a believer? What is an unbelieving believer? Can you relate?

_____

_____

_____

_____

_____

7.   Describe the two kinds of Christians noted in the book. Which one are you?

_____

_____

_____

_____

_____

8.   What are the mountains you face? Do they cause you to be overwhelmed, fearful, and/or worried? What does the book state is the biggest mountain you face? Is this true in your life?

_____

_____

_____

_____

_____

9.   What is true faith in God? How does it relate to your mountains?

_____

_____

_____

_____

_____

10. Read Mark 9:21–24. Can you relate to this man? If so, ask Jesus to heal your unbelief.

_____

_____

_____

_____

11. What do you think about Jesus' statement in Mark 9:23: "All things are possible to him who believes"? Do you believe this for your own life? Why or why not? If not, what will you do about this unbelief in your heart?

_____

_____

_____

_____

_____

GOD'S WORD IS HYDRATION

12. Read Romans 10:17. Where does it say faith comes from?

_____

_____

_____

_____

13. Read John 1:1 and John 1:14. According to these Scriptures, who is the Word?

_____

_____

_____

_____

_____

14. Why are reading and knowing the Bible important? Why are they essential to heart hydration?

_____

_____

_____

_____

_____

15.　How does the concept of "Word in, Word out" work?

_____

_____

_____

_____

16.　Thirty-Day Challenge: I challenge you to apply the "Word in, Word out" concept to your life for thirty days straight and see how it changes your faith. Write a Scripture on a note card or sticky note and post it where you will see it. Every time you see it, read it out loud and speak it to your heart and soul. Do you accept the challenge?

GOD'S FAITHFULNESS IS NOT IN QUESTION

17.　Read Psalm 100:5. What does it say about God? Do you believe this about Him in the depths of your heart and soul? If not, pray and ask Jesus to reset your core belief system.

_____

_____

_____

_____

_____

EXPECTATION

18.　What is against God's character? Why? Do you believe this with all your heart?

_____

_____

_____

_____

_____

WITHOUT WAVERING

19. Read James 1:6–8. What does this Scripture say about those who waver in their faith in God? How can you be fully convinced, without wavering, that God will do all He has promised?

_____

_____

_____

_____

_____

_____

20. Read Ephesians 6:10–19. Why and how do you stand on God's Word?

_____

_____

_____

_____

_____

_____

STRENGTHEN YOUR FAITH

21. Read Romans 4:20–21. Please go over the list under "allow faith to be strengthened" in the book, then pray and ask Jesus what steps you should take. List them.

_____

_____

_____

_____

_____

DO NOT WASTE THE WAIT

22. What closes the gap between promise and fulfillment? What is the opposite of faith?

_____
_____
_____
_____
_____
_____
_____

23. Why is it important to view a waiting time as valuable? Is there something you have been waiting for? Ask Jesus what He wants to accomplish in your heart while you wait.

_____
_____
_____
_____
_____
_____
_____

24. What is the definition of worry? Read Matthew 6:25–34 and Philippians 4:6–7. What do these Scriptures say about worry?

_____
_____
_____
_____
_____
_____

25. List the ways to not waste the wait.

_____

_____

_____

_____

_____

_____

26. List the ways to find beauty in the wait.

_____

_____

_____

_____

_____

_____

27. Examine your faith. If there are areas that need solidify-
     ing, please take steps to heart hydration by purposefully
     strengthening your faith. What steps will you take? And
     please know, strengthening your faith is a journey—enjoy it!

_____

_____

_____

_____

_____

_____

7
A HEART-STYLE OF THANKSGIVING

1. Read 1 Thessalonians 5:18. Why does thankfulness hydrate your heart?

   _____

   _____

   _____

   _____

2. Why is thankfulness God's will? What does thankfulness accomplish in your heart?

   _____

   _____

   _____

   _____

3. Read 1 Corinthians 4:7. How does thankfulness cause your heart and soul to stay humble?

   _____

   _____

   _____

   _____

HEART-STYLE

4. What does it mean to live with thanksgiving, not just as a lifestyle but a heart-style? What is required to live this way?

_____

_____

_____

_____

_____

_____

GIVE THANKS FOR *ALL* THINGS?

5. Read Ephesians 5:20. What does it say about giving thanks? Can you give thanks for *all* things? If not, what will you do to change that?

_____

_____

_____

_____

_____

_____

NO ACCUSATION

6. What causes your heart to stay soft toward Jesus? How does it work?

_____

_____

_____

_____

_____

_____

7.   Read Philippians 4:11–12. How does this Scripture relate to a heart-style of thanksgiving?

_____

_____

_____

_____

PERSPECTIVE CHANGE

8.   How does a change of perspective help hydrate your heart?

_____

_____

_____

_____

9.   What will happen to your heart if you do not change your perspective and acquire a thankful heart?

_____

_____

_____

_____

EVIDENCE

10.   Why is a heart-style of thanksgiving confirmation of true faith in God?

_____

_____

_____

_____

11. Read Hebrews 11:1. What is the evidence of things not seen?

_____

_____

_____

_____

_____

12. A faith-filled life is lived by believing God's Word and applying it to every situation and circumstance. What is the next step after applying God's word?

_____

_____

_____

_____

13. List the three very practical ways to transition your heart and life to a heart-style of thanksgiving.

_____

_____

_____

_____

_____

14. Thirty-Day Challenge: For thirty days straight, do all the steps listed in your answer to #13. At the end of the thirty days, take note of your progress and how your heart has changed.

8
LOVE AND OBEDIENCE

1. What is a huge element to heart hydration?

   _____

   _____

   _____

   _____

2. What does it mean to fear God?

   _____

   _____

   _____

   _____

3. Read Psalm 25:14. What does this Scripture tell you about the fear of the Lord?

   _____

   _____

   _____

   _____

OUR ALL

4.   Read Deuteronomy 10:12 and Mark 12:30. How does the fear of the Lord relate to these Scriptures? What does it mean to you personally to love God with all your heart, soul, mind, and strength?

_____

_____

_____

_____

_____

PRICELESS TREASURE

5.   What is the ultimate treasure the fear of the Lord unlocks?

_____

_____

_____

_____

_____

6.   What is the difference between knowing about God and knowing Him personally?

_____

_____

_____

_____

_____

WHAT?

7.   Read the following Scriptures and fill in the blanks According to these Scriptures, what exactly is the fear of the Lord?

Job 28:28 (NLT): "The fear of the Lord is true_____

_____."

Psalm 19:9 (NKJV): "The fear of the Lord is _____

_____."

Proverbs 1:7 (NLT): "The fear of the Lord is the _____

_____."

Proverbs 14:27 (NKJV): "The fear of the Lord is a _____

_____."

Isaiah 33:6 (NKJV): "The fear of the Lord is _____

_____."

Proverbs 8:13 (NKJV): "The fear of the Lord_____

_____."

Proverbs 3:7–8 (NLT): "Fear the Lord and depart from evil. It will be _____."

WHY?

8. Read Psalm 89:7. Why is the fear of the Lord a gateway to blessing, wisdom, and knowledge?

_____

_____

_____

_____

9. Read Proverbs 2:3. What does this Scripture say about comprehending the fear of the Lord? If you have a difficult time grasping the fear of the Lord, what should you do?

_____

_____

_____

_____

THE FEAR OF THE LORD EQUALS LOVE AND OBEDIENCE

10. Read John 15:14 and 1 John 5:3. According to these Scriptures, how do love and obedience go hand in hand?

_____

_____

_____

_____

_____

11. Why are the following statements true? "Loving God by obeying Him is not laborious or out of reach for a submitted heart and soul. God requiring obedience is a sign of His generous love."

_____

_____

_____

_____

12. Is obedience optional? Why or why not? How do you feel about it?

_____

_____

_____

_____

13. Read Psalm 55:19. How does it apply to you personally?

_____

_____

_____

_____

_____

14.   Read 1 Samuel 15:3–24. In general, what does it say about Saul and about obedience?

_____

_____

_____

_____

THE FEAR OF MAN VERSUS THE FEAR OF THE LORD

15.   What is the fear of man?

_____

_____

_____

_____

_____

_____

16.   Read Proverbs 29:25 and Matthew 10:28. What do these Scriptures tell you about the fear of man? Do you struggle with needing man's approval more that God's? Or are you overly concerned with people's opinion of you? If so, what will you do about it?

_____

_____

_____

_____

_____

_____

_____

17. Please take time to pray and ask God to give you greater understanding of the fear of the Lord and to engrave this biblical principle on your heart. Write your prayer out.

_____

_____

_____

_____

_____

_____

_____

9
HEALING THE HEART AND SOUL

1. Can you relate to life being messy? What happens in the messiness of life?

   _____
   _____
   _____
   _____

2. In the second paragraph of this chapter, what is said about Jesus and the gift of healing?

   _____
   _____
   _____
   _____

HEALING THE INSIDE

3. What does it mean to be wounded?

   _____
   _____
   _____
   _____

4. A natural, common reaction to being wounded and broken-hearted is to fill the emptiness. Why is this a crucial point? What should be done at this time?

_____

_____

_____

_____

_____

_____

5. Can you recognize any areas in your life where you have filled your emptiness with things other than God? What are they? Are you willing to submit them to Jesus and let Him heal you?

_____

_____

_____

_____

_____

_____

6. What are three reasons listed that cause some people to struggle for years on end with the same issues? Why are they seemingly incapable of getting free, even though they have tried for years? Can you relate to any or all of these? If so, what will you do about it?

_____

_____

_____

_____

_____

_____

7.   Why does being wounded lead to numbness? Why is being at the end of yourself a good place to be?

_____

_____

_____

_____

_____

_____

8.   How does blame-shifting delay heart hydration?

_____

_____

_____

_____

_____

9.   How should you view healing and deliverance? Why?

_____

_____

_____

_____

10. List the key components that helped me (the author) heal. What was the most valuable component to my healing? Why?

_____

_____

_____

_____

11. Please take the needed steps to draw nearer to Jesus. I would hate for you to go through all the motions of healing and not engage with the healer Himself—He is the essence of heart hydration.

_____

_____

_____

_____

_____

_____

THE HOLY SPIRIT

12. Read Galatians 5:16, John 4:24, John 14:26, and Ephesians 1:13–15. What do these passages say about the Holy Spirit?

_____

_____

_____

_____

_____

_____

13. What is your relationship with the Holy Spirit? Why do you even need a relationship with the Holy Spirit?

_____

_____

_____

_____

_____

_____

TRUE REPENTANCE

14. Read Isaiah 57:15, Acts 3:19, and Romans 2:4. What do these Scriptures say about repentance? What is repentance?

15. Read Matthew 5:23–24 and James 5:16. What do these Scriptures tell you about confessing your sin? Why does sin need to be confessed to God?

16. Why is it sometimes necessary to confess to someone you can trust and to the people you have sinned against? What does confession do for you?

17. How is the simple act of repentance described?

18. Read 2 Corinthians 7:10. What is godly sorrow? What is the difference between godly sorrow and worldly sorrow? Why do you need godly sorrow?

_____

_____

_____

_____

_____

_____

19. Read Psalm 103:12 and Romans 8:1. What do these Scriptures say about God's forgiveness? Do you need to forgive yourself for anything? If so, do it now.

_____

_____

_____

_____

_____

_____

THE "F" WORD—FORGIVE

20. What are your views on forgiveness? How do you feel about forgiving others no matter what they have done?

_____

_____

_____

_____

_____

21. Read Mark 11:26. What does this Scripture say about for-
    giveness and about God forgiving you? Do you think for-
    giveness is optional?

    _____

    _____

    _____

    _____

    _____

22. What is the foremost aspect to remember about forgiveness?

    _____

    _____

    _____

    _____

    _____

23. Do you need a change of heart regarding forgiveness? If so,
    pray now and make the exchange.

    _____

    _____

    _____

    _____

    _____

24. Make a list of people you need to forgive. Pray and ask Jesus
    to help you forgive the people on the list.

    _____

    _____

    _____

    _____

LIBERATE

25. What is the meaning of the word "deliverance"?

_____

_____

_____

_____

_____

26. Read Psalm 18:2. List the seven characteristics of God in this Scripture. How does this make you feel about Him?

_____

_____

_____

_____

_____

27. Read Luke 4:18. What does this Scripture tell you about Jesus in regards to deliverance? Why does deliverance bring a flood of heart hydration?

_____

_____

_____

_____

_____

28. What is the answer to everything? What is one tool Jesus uses to set people free?

_____

_____

_____

_____

_____

29. Read Romans 6:16. What are strongholds? How are they acquired? How does this Scripture relate to strongholds?

_____

_____

_____

_____

_____

30. Read 2 Corinthians 10:4. What does this Scripture tell you about strongholds?

_____

_____

_____

_____

_____

31. Go over the list of common strongholds. Prayerfully make a list of those you struggle with.

_____

_____

_____

_____

_____

32. What are the four ways listed for dealing with strongholds?

_____

_____

_____

_____

_____

33.   After you recognize strongholds in your life, you may want to seek your pastor or a spiritually grounded friend to pray with you. Or you can follow the simple procedure in the book. Please read the entirety of the chapter 9 "Healing the Heart and Soul" before proceeding with praying deliverance prayers. If you deal with sexual issues, please wait until you read chapter 10 on "Healing Sexual Brokenness," then proceed with praying deliverance prayers.

This is a suggested prayer. You can pray this one or make up your own. It does not need to be a formal ritual, but it does need to be sincere.

Jesus, I recognize _____ to be a stronghold in my life. I repent and ask forgiveness for allowing it to influence my life. In Jesus name I renounce _____. I break its power over my mind, will, and emotions, over my heart, spirit, and body, over my past and my future. I exchange the stronghold of _____ for _____. I choose to forgive _____. Jesus, fill me with Your healing presence. Go deep into the root cause and heal this place with Your love, forgiveness, and acceptance. Thank you that because of Your sacrifice on the cross, I am free. Strengthen me and my faith to stand strong and remember who I am in You. Amen.

DETAILS

34.   Read Ephesians 6:12 and Colossians 2:15. What do they tell you about principalities and the battles we face? Should you be afraid of principalities? Why or why not?

_____

_____

_____

_____

UNHEALTHY CONNECTIONS

35. What is an unhealthy connection? Why can it dehydrate your heart and damage your relationship with Jesus?

_____

_____

_____

_____

_____

_____

36. How does an unhealthy connection form?

_____

_____

_____

_____

_____

37. Please read all of chapter 9 before praying the following prayer. Prayerfully make a list of the people you have unhealthy connections with and want freedom from that are not sexual. Then proceed to pray the following prayer. If all your unhealthy connections are sexual, wait until you read chapter 10 on "Healing Sexual Brokenness," and instead use the prayer at the end of that chapter.

_____

_____

_____

_____

_____

_____

Jesus, I repent and ask forgiveness for establishing and maintaining this connection. In Jesus' name, I sever this unhealthy connection with _____. I break it over my heart, my mind, will, and emotions, my spirit, and my body. I sever this tie over my memory, over my past, and over my future. Forgive me for allowing this relationship to influence me in an unhealthy way. I choose to forgive _____. I submit to You. Fill me with Your love. Amen.

HEALING THE ROOT CAUSE

38. Describe a root cause. Why is it important to deal with root causes?

_____

_____

_____

_____

_____

_____

39. Can you identify any root causes related to your list of strongholds or ties? What is the procedure used to heal the heart and soul at the root cause? List the procedure and prayerfully use it to deal with your root causes. (Note: If your issues are sexual, wait until you read chapter 10 on "Healing Sexual Brokenness" before using this procedure.)

_____

_____

_____

_____

_____

_____

CONTEND FOR YOUR FREEDOM

40.   What is extremely important to do after praying deliverance prayers? How do you fill up and contend?

_____

_____

_____

_____

_____

_____

41.   Read John 8:36. Why is believing this Scripture essential to living free? What should you do when the enemy tries to harass you?

_____

_____

_____

_____

_____

_____

42.   Read Philippians 3:3. What does this Scripture tell you about Christ in regard to human effort? How does the truth of Philippians 3:3 make you feel?

_____

_____

_____

_____

_____

_____

43. Is temptation a sin? What should you do with temptations? How does submission and James 4:6–8 help you deal with temptation?

_____

_____

_____

_____

_____

44. What is another method you can use when struggling with temptation or when God reveals an empty place in your heart, soul, or life? How does this method work?

_____

_____

_____

_____

_____

NOURISH YOUR HEART AND SOUL

45. What is one of the best ways to contend for freedom and to continually live in close relationship with Jesus?

_____

_____

_____

_____

_____

46. How is feeding the heart and soul equal to feeding the body?

_____

_____

_____

_____

A CONTINUOUS WORK

47. Why is healing something you can continually access? What method can be used for this? Seek to make this simple practice a staple in your life.

_____

_____

_____

_____

_____

_____

OFFENSES

48. Read Corinthians 13:5 and Philippians 1:10. What do these two Scriptures tell you about offenses?

_____

_____

_____

_____

_____

_____

49. Is being offended a choice? Why or why not? List two ways to deal with offenses. How do submission and believing that Jesus is enough help you deal with offenses?

_____

_____

_____

_____

_____

_____

50. Stepping into healing is a choice. What choice will you make in regards to deliverance prayers, breaking strongholds and unhealthy connections, root causes, and offenses? Remember who you are in Christ, and keep in mind—freedom is a staple for those who follow Christ.

_____

_____

_____

_____

_____

10

HEALING SEXUAL BROKENNESS

Please take what you just read from the previous chapter and combine it with what you learn from this chapter to acquire a complete understanding of sexual healing.

1. How do you think Jesus views sexual sin and sexual brokenness?

_____

_____

_____

_____

_____

2. How does Jesus extend grace regarding sexual sin and sexual brokenness?

_____

_____

_____

_____

_____

3.   Read Psalm 51:17. What are the two kinds of brokenness? Why is one good to have and why does the other require healing?

_____

_____

_____

_____

_____

_____

4.   Sexual brokenness cannot be dismissed because a person does not have apparent sexual problems. Make a list of outward forms of sexual brokenness mentioned. Do you struggle with any of these issues? Are any of your issues related to sexual sin or sexual brokenness?

_____

_____

_____

_____

_____

_____

THE UNMENTIONABLES

5.   If the subject of sexual healing makes you uncomfortable, what should you do?

_____

_____

_____

_____

_____

AND SO IT BEGAN

6. What does the cloak allegory represent? Can you relate to putting on or wearing the cloak?

_____
_____
_____
_____
_____
_____

THE HEALING PROCESS

7. How does the healing process usually begin?

_____
_____
_____
_____
_____

8. What is the meaning of the following passage and how does it apply to you? "When the process begins, it is common to feel as if your life is unraveling. What is really important to keep in mind is that it is just a season. It will not last forever; therefore, you must resolve to stay with it."

_____
_____
_____
_____
_____

9. Read Matthew 18:21–35. Why is forgiveness essential to sexual healing? What does this Scripture say to you about forgiveness?

_____

_____

_____

_____

_____

_____

SEX TIES YOU TO ANOTHER PERSON

10. Read Ephesians 5:31. How does this Scripture relate to an unhealthy sexual connection? Why is it important to break an ungodly sexual connection off your heart and soul?

_____

_____

_____

_____

_____

_____

11. If you need to sever unhealthy sexual connections, first make a list of all the people you need to disconnect yourself from (you can burn it afterwards!). At the end of this chapter is a prayer you can pray to sever unhealthy sexual connections.

_____

_____

_____

_____

_____

_____

SEX IS MORE THAN SKIN TO SKIN

12.   Read 1 Corinthians 6:16–20 in *The Message*. List the nine points mentioned from this Scripture. Can you see from this passage how sexual sin affects your whole person: body, soul, heart, and spirit, past, present, and future?

_____

_____

_____

_____

_____

FEAR IS A BULLY

13.   List the reasons why some people still live with a dehydrated heart and soul, holding tight to their cloak of sexual brokenness.

_____

_____

_____

_____

_____

14.   Why is fear a bully? Do you recognize it working in your own life? Where? What will you do about it?

_____

_____

_____

_____

_____

15. Can you relate to any of the reasons given for not choosing to step into healing? If so, list them, then be sure to pray and break the stronghold of fear off your life.

_____

_____

_____

_____

_____

_____

16. How much power does fear really have? Read 2 Timothy 1:7. What does it say about your reality as a believer in Christ?

_____

_____

_____

_____

_____

PRAYER TO SEVER UNHEALTHY SEXUAL CONNECTIONS

17. The next step is to sever unhealthy sexual connections, and I have included a prayer to help as you take this step, which you can tailor to fit your individual situation. You can pray alone or with a pastor, family member, or friend who understands this manner of prayer. It is very important to remember after severing each connection to invite Jesus into the place where the tie has been severed, asking Him to heal and fill you.

Jesus, please forgive me for my inappropriate behavior with _____. Forgive me for linking my heart, soul, body, and affections with _____. I truly am sorry for the damage I have caused my own heart, soul, body, and spirit. I see that my sin was not only against You but against my whole person and my future. Thank you that the power of the cross has healed and delivered me from the root causes of my sin. Today I step into this truth.

I renounce and sever every connection with _____. I sever it over my heart, mind, will, emotions, body, spirit, my past, and my future. I forgive _____ and all involved. I forgive myself. Forgive me for finding my self-worth, identity, and value from this person's view and acceptance of me. I disconnect myself from the person I was at that time and from the tie of who I used to be. I am no longer that weak, immature, hurt, fragmented, grasping person. I am free, forgiven, pure, and maturing daily. Strengthen me and my faith to stand firm in your grace and in the truth of who I am. Thank you, Jesus! Amen .

STEP INTO HIS HEALING LOVE

18. List the thirteen points summarizing the healing process. If any of this is unclear, please reread the section you need clarity on so you may gain a greater understanding of this healing process.

_____

_____

_____

_____

_____

_____

_____

_____

_____

19. What are you thinking right now? (Write out your thoughts.) Is Jesus in His faithfulness tugging at your heart? Is He gently pressing tender forgotten areas of your past, wanting to heal you? Maybe your wounds are not sexual, but you still may need healing. Please do not shrug God off. Take this opportunity to seek Jesus and ask Him to reveal areas of brokenness, sexual or otherwise, in your heart and soul. Jesus has so generously provided healing hydration and freedom for you.

_____

_____

_____

_____

_____

_____

_____

_____

20. Proceed with your healing process. What will your first step be?

_____

_____

_____

_____

_____

_____

_____

_____

11

YOU'VE GOT THIS

1. Read Psalm 23. As you read it, savor every word. Take it in and realize this is your portion in life.

2. Read Hebrews 11:4 in The Message. According to this Scripture, what catches God's attention? How does this apply to you?

   _____

   _____

   _____

3. Read Isaiah 55:1–3. I encourage and challenge you to accept the invitation of this passage.

4. Are you thirsty for heart hydration? Are you ready to step into the grace of God? Are you ready to step into every provision the cross bought for you?

   _____

   _____

   _____

Go ahead—you've got this!
Do not delay. He is waiting.

NOTES

NOTES

NOTES

NOTES

NOTES

NOTES

NOTES

NOTES

NOTES

NOTES

NOTES

NOTES

NOTES

NOTES

NOTES

NOTES

NOTES

NOTES

Made in the USA
San Bernardino, CA
20 May 2018